First Steps in Reading English

I. A. Richards / Christine Gibson

Level 1
(1000-word)

IBC パブリッシング

FIRST STEPS IN READING ENGLISH

Copyright © 1957, by Language Research, Inc.

The above copyright was transferred to the President and Fellows of Harvard College (Harvard University) in 1996.

All rights reserved.

Printed and distributed in Japan by arrangement with Language Research, Inc.

*本書は、洋販出版刊『絵で見る英語の第一歩』を改題したものです。元はGraded Direct Method用に開発されたリーディング教材のひとつで、英国Cambridge大学のC. K. Ogden によるBasic Englishをベースにしています。

はじめに

　ラダーシリーズは、「はしご (ladder)」を使って一歩一歩上を目指すように、学習者の実力に合わせ、無理なくステップアップできるよう開発された英文リーダーのシリーズです。

　リーディング力をつけるためには、繰り返したくさん読むこと、いわゆる「多読」がもっとも効果的な学習法であると言われています。多読では、「1. 速く 2. 訳さず英語のまま 3. なるべく辞書を使わず」に読むことが大切です。スピードを計るなど、速く読むよう心がけましょう（たとえば TOEIC® テストの音声スピードはおよそ1分間に150語です）。そして1語ずつ訳すのではなく、英語を英語のまま理解するくせをつけるようにします。こうして読み続けるうちに語感がついてきて、だんだんと英語が理解できるようになるのです。まずは、ラダーシリーズの中からあなたのレベルに合った本を選び、少しずつ英文に慣れ親しんでください。たくさんの本を手にとるうちに、英文書がすらすら読めるようになってくるはずです。

《本シリーズの特徴》

- 中学校レベルから中級者レベルまで5段階に分かれています。自分に合ったレベルからスタートしてください。
- クラシックから現代文学、ノンフィクション、ビジネスと幅広いジャンルを扱っています。あなたの興味に合わせてタイトルを選べます。
- 巻末のワードリストで、いつでもどこでも単語の意味を確認できます。レベル1、2では、文中の全ての単語が、レベル3以上は中学校レベル外の単語が掲載されています。
- カバーにヘッドホーンマークのついているタイトルは、オーディオ・サポートがあります。ウェブから購入／ダウンロードし、リスニング教材としても併用できます。

《使用語彙について》

レベル1：中学校で学習する単語約1000語

レベル2：レベル1の単語＋使用頻度の高い単語約300語

レベル3：レベル1の単語＋使用頻度の高い単語約600語

レベル4：レベル1の単語＋使用頻度の高い単語約1000語

レベル5：語彙制限なし

Contents

First Steps in Reading English ... *1*

Letter Intake of First Steps in Reading English ... *153*

Index ... *155*

Word List ... *164*

First Steps in Reading English

読みはじめる前に

「英語が読める」とはどのようなことをいうのでしょうか。

あなたは"Thank you"や"Hello"と言うとき、日本語に訳していますか。「ありがとう」「こんにちは」といちいち訳さなくても、そのまま意味が理解できていると思います。このように、英文を日本語に訳さずにそのまま受け入れて理解することが、ここで言う「英語を読む」ということです。

この本は、たくさんのイラストとシンプルな文で構成されています。アルファベット7文字だけを使ったごく簡単な内容から始まり、単語の数が増えるにつれて登場するアルファベットも増えていきます。脚注には、それまでに習ったアルファベットが全て並べられています。同じ語や表現を繰り返し使って、少しずつより複雑な内容を学んでいけるように注意深く書かれているのです。

この本を読むときは、イメージを豊かにして、頭の中で「日本語に訳さない」ように気をつけてください。イラストがそれぞれの文の意味をわかりやすく示していますので、途中で知らない単語や表現が出てきたとしても、意味を間違えたりすることなく正しいイメージを持って読み進めることができます。

英語初心者の方からある程度英語を学んできた人まで、英語を読むための基礎的な方法を、無理なく身につけることができるでしょう。

この本を読み終わる頃には、あなたもきっと英語が読めるようになっているはずです。

巻末のワードリストは、読んでいてどうしてもわからないときのための非常用です。できる限り使わないようにしましょう。

FIRST STEPS IN READING ENGLISH

This is a man.

This is a hat.

This hat is his hat.

This is his hat.

a b c d e f g **h i** j k l **m n** o p q r **s t** u v w x y z

First Steps in Reading English

This is a hat.

It is this man's hat.

It is his hat.

This hat is his hat.

——— That is a hat.

It is that man's hat.

It is a hat.

——— That hat is his hat.

a b c d e f g **h i** j k l **m n** o p q r **s t** u v w x y z

First Steps in Reading English

This is a man.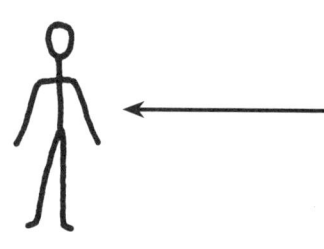

This is a name.

TIM SMITH

It is this man's name.

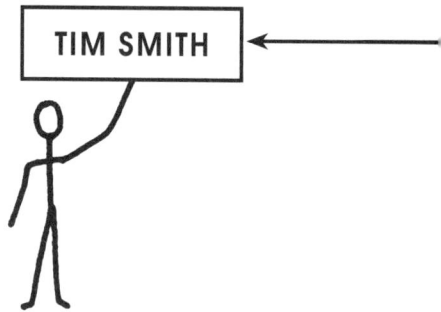

This is his name,

Tim Smith.

---

a b c d e f g h i j k l m n o p q r s t u v w x y z

4

———— That is a man.

———— That is a name.

———— That name is his name.

———— That is his name.

---

a b c d e f g h i j k l m n o p q r s t u v w x y z

This is Tim.

He is Tim Smith.

Tim's name is Tim Smith.

> TIM SMITH

Tim's name is Tim.

---

a b c d **e** f g **h i** j k l **m n** o p q r **s t** u v w x y z

This is Ann.

She is Ann Smith.

Ann's name is Ann Smith.

ANN SMITH

Ann's name is Ann.

TIM SMITH

This name is Tim Smith's.

It is Tim Smith's name.

This is Tim Smith's hat.

It is Tim's hat.

a b c d e f g h i j k l m n o p q r s t u v w x y z

ANN SMITH

This name is Ann Smith's.

It is Ann Smith's name.

This is Ann Smith's hat.

It is Ann's hat.

a b c d e f g h i j k l m n o p q r s t u v w x y z

FIRST STEPS IN READING ENGLISH

This is a hat.

This is a hat.

This hat is Tim's hat.

It is Tim's hat.

Tim's name is in it.

a b c d e f g h i j k l m n o p q r s t u v w x y z

This is a hat.

This is a hat.

This hat is Ann's hat.

It is Ann's hat.

Ann's name is in it.

a b c d e f g h i j k l m n o p q r s t u v w x y z

First Steps in Reading English

This is a man.

This is a hand.

This hand is his hand.

It is his hand.

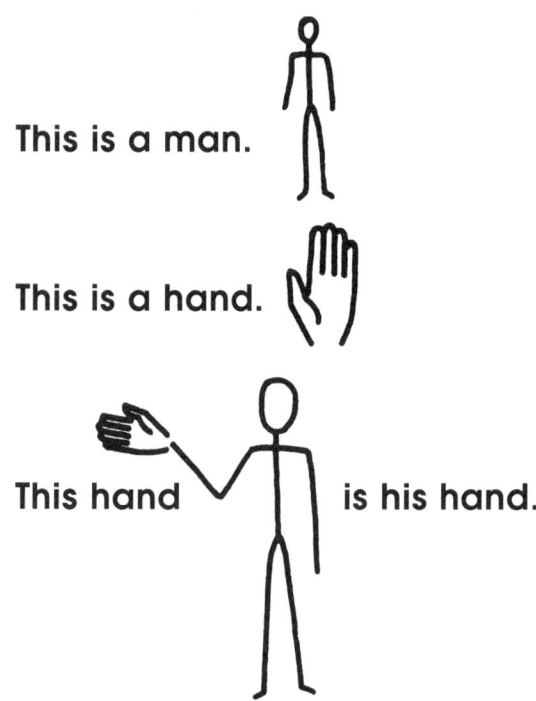

a b c d e f g h i j k l m n o p q r s t u v w x y z

FIRST STEPS IN READING ENGLISH

This is a man.

This is a head.

This head is his head.

It is his head.

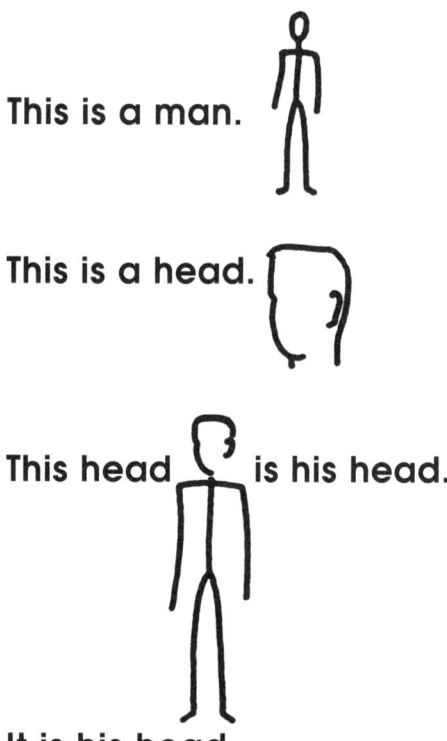

a b c d e f g h i j k l m n o p q r s t u v w x y z

This is a man.

This is his hand
and this is his hand.

This is his head.

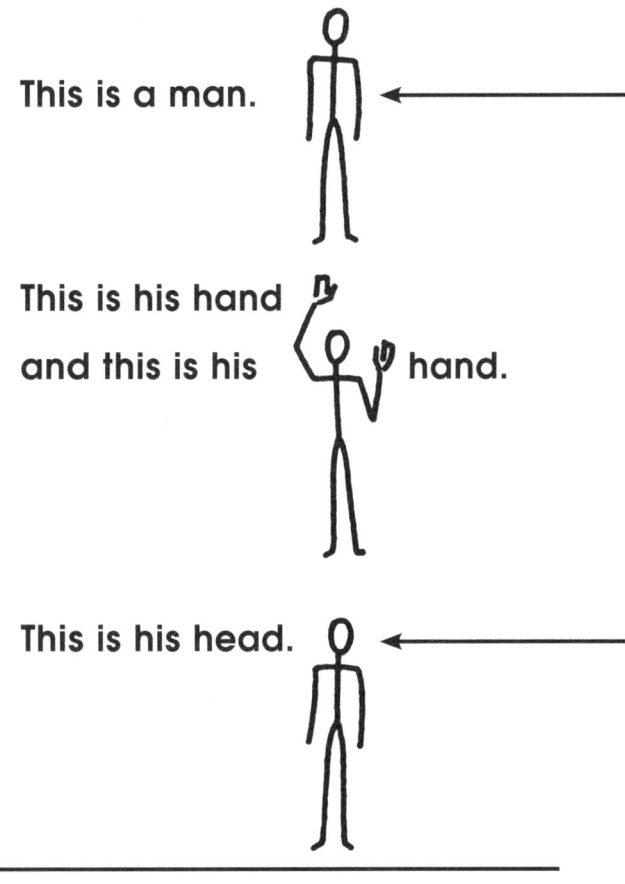

a b c d e f g h i j k l m n o p q r s t u v w x y z

That is a man.

That is his hand
and that is his hand.

That is his head.

a b c d e f g h i j k l m n o p q r s t u v w x y z

This is a hat and this is a hand.

The hat is in the hand.

It is in the hand.

That hand is in a hat.

---

a b c d e f g h i j k l m n o p q r s t u v w x y z

This is a hand and this is a hat.

The hand is in the hat.

It is in the hat.

That hat is in a hand.

a b c d e f g h i j k l m n o p q r s t u v w x y z

This is a head

and this is a
head.

This is a man's head.

It is a man's head.

It is this man's head.

a b c d e f g h i j k l m n o p q r s t u v w x y z

This is a hand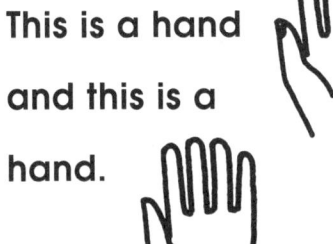

and this is a

hand.

This is a man's hand.

It is a man's hand.

It is that man's hand.

It is his hand.

---

a b c d e f g h i j k l m n o p q r s t u v w x y z

This is a hand.

These are hands.

This is a head.

These are heads.

This is a seat.

These are a man's hands.

These are a man's hats.

a b c d e f g h i j k l m n o p q r s t u v w x y z

First Steps in Reading English

This is a man.

These are men.

This is a hat.

These are hats.

These are seats.

This is a
man's hat.

These are
men's heads.

a b c d e f g h i j k l m n o p q r s t u v w x y z

This is an ear.

It is a man's ear.

It is Tim Smith's ear.

This is an arm.

It is his arm.

This is his ear

and these

are his arms.

---

a b c d e f g h i j k l m n o p q r s t u v w x y z

These are ears.

The ears are Ann's.

These are arms.

The arms are her arms.

This is Ann's ear
and this

is her arm.

First Steps in Reading English

That man is there.

This man is here.

This man is Tim.

He is Tim Smith.

TIM SMITH

Tim's name is here.

Ned's name is there.

---

a b c d e f g h i j k l m n o p q r s t u v w x y z

That man is there.

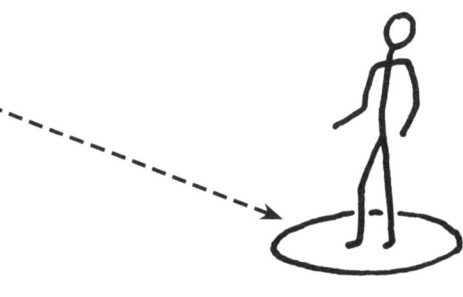

This man is here.

This man is Ned.

He is Ned Reed.

| NED REED |

Ned's name is here.

Tim's name is there.

---

a b c d e f g h i j k l m n o p q r s t u v w x y z

Here are Tim and Ann.

Here are their hands.

These are Tim's hands

and these are Ann's.

Ann's hands are

in Tim's hands.

---

a b c **d e** f g **h i** j k l **m n** o p q **r s t** u v w x y z

First Steps in Reading English

Here are Tim and Ann.

Ann's hand is in Tim's hand.

His hand is in hers and

her hand is in his.

Tim and Ann are

hand in hand.

---

a b c d e f g h i j k l m n o p q r s t u v w x y z

This is a rat.

This is its head.

These are its ears.

This is a hair.

These are hairs.

This is a hat.

A rat is in it.

This is the hat.

This is the rat.

It is in the air.

a b c d e f g h i j k l m n o p q r s t u v w x y z

Here are Tim and Ann.

Tim is here.

Ann is there.

She is in the air.

Here is Ann.

Tim is there.

He is in the air.

This is Ann's hair.

It is in the air.

This is a hair.

These are three hairs.

This is Tim's hair.

It is his hair.

a b c d e f g h i j k l m n o p q r s t u v w x y z

This is a train.

A man is in the train.

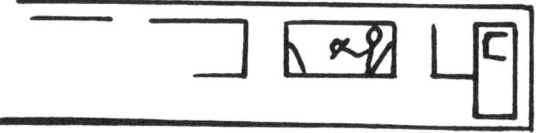

He is in the train.

He is in it.

His hat is in his hand.

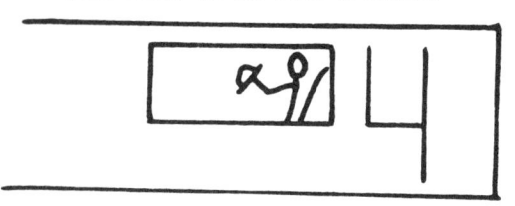

a b c d e f g h i j k l m n o p q r s t u v w x y z

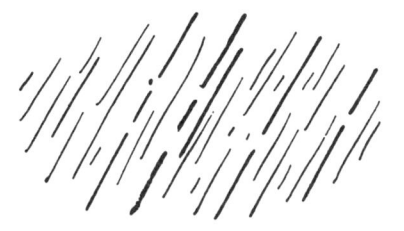

This is rain.

A man is in the rain.

He is in the rain.

He is in it.

Is his hat in his hand?

a b c d e f g h i j k l m n o p q r s t u v w x y z

FIRST STEPS IN READING ENGLISH

This man is

Mr. Reed.

He is Ned Reed.

His name is Ned Reed.

This is his name.

NED REED

Mr. Reed is here.

a b c d e f g h i j k l m n o p q r s t u v w x y z

This is

Mrs. Reed.

She is Ida Reed.

Her name is Ida Reed.

This is her name.

> IDA REED

Ida and Ned Reed are here.

Are Mr. and Mrs.

Reed here?

This is Miss Hart

and this is Miss Hart

and this is Miss Hart.

These are the three Miss Harts.

This is Miss Hester Hart.

This is Miss Enid Hart.

This is Miss Esther Hart.

Hester, Enid and Esther

are sisters.

a b c d e f g h i j k l m n o p q r s t u v w x y z

This is Mr. Sands,

this is Mr. Tedder

and this is Mr. Sims.

These men's names are

| ERNEST SANDS |
| NAT TEDDER |
| SAM SIMS |

This is Sam's hand.

This is Nat's head.

This is Ernest's ear.

Ernest, Nat and Sam are Mr.

Sands, Mr. Tedder and Mr. Sims.

a b c d e f g h i j k l m n o p q r s t u v w x y z

Miss Hester, Miss Enid and

Miss Esther Hart are sisters.

Their name is the same, Hart.

Hester is Enid's and

Esther's sister.

Enid is Hester's and

Esther's sister.

Esther is Hester's and

Enid's sister.

Is Esther Hester's sister?

Is Enid Hester's sister?

Is Hester Esther's sister?

---

a b c d e f g h i j k l m n o p q r s t u v w x y z

Here is a tree

and here is a tree

and here is a tree.

These are three trees.

The trees are ash trees.

Their name is the same.

> Three trees and
>
> three trees and
>
> three trees are
>
> nine trees.

a b c d e f g h i j k l m n o p q r s t u v w x y z

This man's hat is
on his head.
That man's hat is
in his hand.

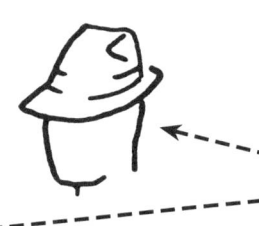

These hats are on a seat.

This man's hat is in his hand.

That man's hat is on his head.

It is on his head.

Those hats are on that seat.

a b c d e f g h i j k l m n o p q r s t u v w x y z

Here are Mr. Smith

and his son.

The son's name is Tom.

It is Tom.

It is not Tim.

Tom is Tim Smith's son.

Here is Tom's name.

> TOM SMITH

Tim and his son are hand

in hand.

Here are Ann Smith and her mother.

Ann's hand is in her mother's hand.

Ann's name and her mother's name are the same.

| ANN SMITH | ANN SMITH |

Ann is Tom's sister.

a b c d e f g h i j k l m n o p q r s t u v w x y z

This is Ann.

A tooth is in her hand.

It is her tooth.

It is not in her head.

These are teeth.

a b c d e f g h i j k l m n o p q r s t u v w x y z

FIRST STEPS IN READING ENGLISH

This is Tom.

This is his hair.

These are his ears.

This is his nose.

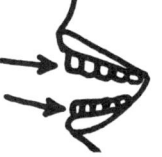

These are his teeth.

a b c d e f g h i j k l m n o p q r s t u v w x y z

This is Tom's train.

This is Tom's station.

The train is not in the station.

There is no train in the station.

That is Ann on her horse, Otto. - - - - -

a b c **d** e f g **h i** j k l **m n** o p q **r s t** u v w x y z

Here is Ann's room.

Ann is in her room.

Here she is on her horse, Otto.

Ann's horse's name is Otto.

a b c d e f g h i j k l m n o p q r s t u v w x y z

This is Mr. Smith's room.

He is in his room.

He is at the door.

His hand is on the door.

Mrs. Smith is not in the room.

She is in another room.

Mrs. Smith is here.

This is her room.

Tom's shirt is in her hand.

Tom is at her side.

The shirt is Tom's shirt.

This is another shirt.

Here are three horses.

Here are their noses.

Three noses

and three noses

and three noses

are nine noses.

Here is one horse.

This is its nose.

Here are nine horses.

Nine horses and one horse are ten horses.

$\dfrac{9}{10}$

a b c d e f g h i j k l m n o p q r s t u v w x y z

This is a shoe.

Here are Tom's shoes.

This is one shoe

and this is

his other shoe.

Here are Mr. Smith's shoes.

a b c d e f g h i j k l m n o p q r s t u v w x y z

This is a dress.

It is Ann's dress.

Here is another dress.

It is her mother's dress.

Here are Ann's other dresses.

abcdefghijklmnopqrstuvwxyz

This is a woman.
She is at a window.

Now another woman is with her.
The two women are at the window.

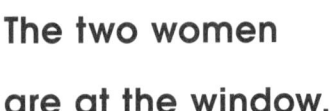

A man is at that other window.

a b c d e f g h i j k l m n o p q r s t u v w x y z

There is the moon and

there are some stars.

This man is at his window.

Those two women are

at their window.

The man and the women are

at their windows.

That is a star.

That is the moon.

There is another star

and three others

and nine others

and ten others.

Here are Tom and Ann.

a b c d e f g h i j k l m n o p q r s t u v w x y z

What is this?

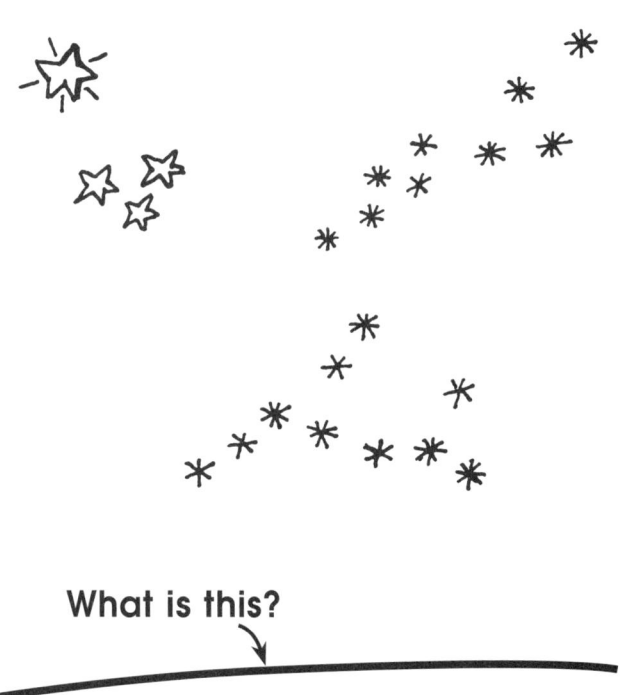

It is the earth.

a b c d e f g h i j k l m n o p q r s t u v w x y z

This man's hat

is in the air.

It was on his head.

Where is his hat now?

There it is.

It is in a tree.

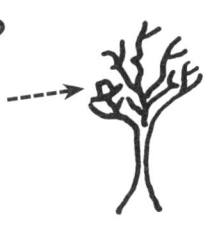

It is not on his head.

Are his hands on his head?

Who is this?

It is Tom.

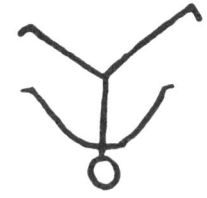

He is on his head.

Now he is not on his head.

He is on his hands.

Now he is on one hand.

And now he is
on the other hand.

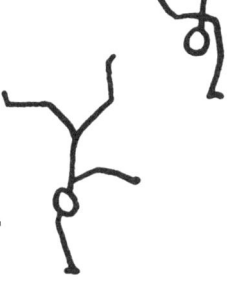

This is a town.

It is near the sea.

That is the sea.

This is a street in the town.

There are other streets in the town.

---

a b c d e f g h i j k l m n o p q r s t u v w x y z

This is not the same town.

It is another town.

It is not near the sea.

This is a road to the town.

Those are trees at the roadside.

Who is this?

It is Miss Hester Hart.

She is with Mr. and Mrs. Smith.

Now she is with Tom and Ann Smith.

a b c d e f g h i j k l m n o p q r s t u v w x y z

Miss Hart was with
Mr. and Mrs. Smith.

She was there with them.
Where is she now?

She is with their son, Tom,
and his sister, Ann.

She is there with them.
That is where she is.

---

a b c d e f g h i j k l m n o p q r s t u v w x y z

Where is Miss Hart now?

Where is Hester?

Here she is.

What is this?

It is a horse.

It is Hester's horse.

What is her horse's name?

It is Diamond.

---

a b c d e f g h i j k l m n o p q r s t u v w x y z

Where is Hester now?

She is on her horse

on a road.

It is the road to the town

near the sea.

Hester is not in the town.

She is on the road to the town.

a b c d e f g h i j k l m n o p q r s t u v w x y z

What is this?

It is a room with men and women in it.

There are two doors and one window in it.

Two women and three men are in the room.

a b c d e f g h i j k l m n o p q r s t u v w x y z

What is this?

TO THE TRAINS

It is a station.

Those are seats.

There are three women on one seat and on the other are two men.

There is a train in the station.

a b c d e f g h i j k l m n o p q r s t u v w x y z

This is the moon

and these are stars.

This is the new moon.

This is Hester's new hat.

It was in a window in

a store in the town.

The new hat store

It is on Hester's

head now.

a b c d e f g h i j k l m n o p q r s t u v w x y z

First Steps in Reading English

Here is one word. `hat`

Here is another word. `at`

Here are two words. `what` `that`

This is a new word. `word`

These are new words. `word` `new`

These are not new words. `in` `no` `on`

---

a b c d e f g h i j k l m n o p q r s t u v w x y z

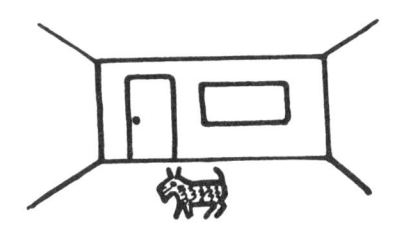

This is a dog.

It is in a room.

This is its head.

These are its ears.

This is its nose.

Here are its teeth.

Its teeth are white.

a b c d e f g h i j k l m n o p q r s t u v w x y z

Now the dog is not in the room. He is in a street.

This is a winter night.

The street and the trees are white with snow.

This is a snowman.
Snow is white.

a b c d e f g h i j k l m n o p q r s t u v w x y z

This is a garden.

This is grass.

Those are trees in the garden.

The dog is in the garden now.

It was in the room.

Now it is on the grass

in the garden.

---

a b c d e f g h i j k l m n o p q r s t u v w x y z

Now Ann and Tom are in the garden with the dog. It is their dog.

The grass and the trees are green.

The air is warm.

It is a warm morning.

---

a b c d e f g h i j k l m n o p q r s t u v w x y z

This is the sea.

Here is a seat.

Tim and his son and the two Anns are on the seat together.

The air is good.

It is warm.

The sea is smooth.

Here is the rain.

There are the Smiths in the room with the wide window. The other side of the window is wet with rain but it is not wet in the room. There is no rain inside the room. The dog is at the door. He is not inside the room. He is wet. He is in the rain.

a b c d e f g h i j k l m n o p q r s t u v w x y z

It is a good morning.

The Smiths are in the water.

The water is warm.

The air is warm.

The sea is smooth.

The dog is in the water with Tom and his sister. Tom and Ann and their dog are wet, but not with rain.

The water is sea water.

a b c d e f g h i j k l m n o p q r s t u v w x y z

Now Ann and Tom are on the sand near the water with their dog. The air is good. Ann's hair is wet and the dog's hair is wet. Tom is not wet.

Their mother is on the warm sand. Her hands and arms and head are on the sand. Mr. Smith is at her side. He is with her. Mr. and Mrs. Smith are together.

This is a bedroom.

There is a bed in it.

There are two doors.

One door is between the bedroom and a bathroom.

The bed is between this door and the window.

abcdefghijklmnopqrstuvwxyz

This is a bathroom.

This is the bath.

It is eight in the morning. There is water in the bath. Tom is in his bath. One arm is in the air. It is his right arm.

a b c d e f g h i j k l m n o p q r s t u v w x y z

Here is Ann with her brother, Tom. What is in this store?

There are two dresses, a shirt and some shoes in the window.

The dresses are red and green.

The shirt is white.

Dresses and shoes are things.

A shirt is a thing.

Ann and her brother are not things.

---

a b c d e f g h i j k l m n o p q r s t u v w x y z

Here are some things in this garden.

What are these things?
There are three trees, two seats and a hat in the garden.
There are two stones and a bone on the grass. A stone is a thing. Bones are things. Tom and his sister are not things.

a b c d e f g h i j k l m n o p q r s t u v w x y z

First Steps in Reading English

There are three letters.   d   g   o

Here is a new letter.   l
The other letters are old letters.
Is the new letter in this word?
No, it is not.

| dog |

The new letter is in this word. It is between <u>o</u> and <u>d</u>.

| old |

a b c d e f g h i j k l m n o p q r s t u v w x y z

There are the letters   l   o

in the word "long."   n   g

There is a tail on

this letter.   g

Here is a dog with

a long tail.

The dog's legs are

long and its tail is long.

Here is a dog with short legs

and a short tail.

---

a b c d e f g h i j k l m n o p q r s t u v w x y z

This is a head.

It is a bird's head.

Here is the bird.

It is on its eggs.

Here are the eggs.

This is an egg.

The eggs are green.

---

a b c d e f g h i j k l m n o p q r s t u v w x y z

The bird was on its eggs.

It was there.

Now it is not on its eggs.

It is here.

It will be on its eggs again.

Here it is on its eggs again.

It is on them again.

abcdefghijklmnopqrstuvwxyz

Here is Miss Enid Hart.

What is that

in her hand?

It is a bag.

What is in the bag?

There is some bread in it.

This bread is in Enid's

hand.

---

a b c d e f g h i j k l m n o p q r s t u v w x y z

This is the bread that was in
Miss Hart's hand.
It is on the grass now.

This is the bird
that was on its
eggs. It is in
the air now. It will be on the
grass. The grass is green.

The bird is white and the bread
is white.

---

a b c d e f g h i j k l m n o p q r s t u v w x y z

Ann and another girl are with Tom in the garden. Tom is on the wall. One leg is on this side. His other leg is on the other side. There is a ball in his right hand. His other hand is on the wall.

abcdefghijklmnopqrstuvwxyz

Ann is short.
Her dress is short.
Her legs are short.
Her arms are short.
She is small.
She is a small girl.

The other girl is not short.
She is tall. Her arms and
legs are long. Her dress
is not short. It is long.
She is a tall girl.

---

a b c d e f g h i j k l m n o p q r s t u v w x y z

A dog is an animal. Horses, rats and goats are animals. These animals are in a line. There is no dog in the line.

The horses' and the rats' tails are long. The two animals at the tail end are goats. Goats and horses and rats and dogs are animals.

---

a b c d e f g h i j k l m n o p q r s t u v w x y z

Some animals are small and some are not.
A rat is a small animal.
Its legs are short.
A horse's legs are long.

These two animals' heads are together. The animals are goats. Their heads are together. Their horns are short.
Some goats' horns are short and some are long.

---

abcdefghijklmnopqrstuvwxyz

Here are two men in a boat.

The boat is on the water. The water is green. There are sea birds on the water. It is morning.

This is a sea bird.
This is its tail.

These are its legs.

Its wings are wide.

---

a b c d e f g h i j k l m n o p q r s t u v w x y z

Now the boat is on the sand.

There is the old moon and one star. No one is in the boat now. Where are the men? The men are in their beds. There is no one in the boat now.

abcdefghijklmnopqrstuvwxyz

These are two islands in the sea.

The islands are small.

There are two tall trees on one of them. The grass on it is green.

Here are Tom and Ann on the other island.

a b c d e f g h i j k l m n o p q r s t u v w x y z

There are two boats on the water.

Ann and Tom are with a man in one boat. The three are together in the man's boat.

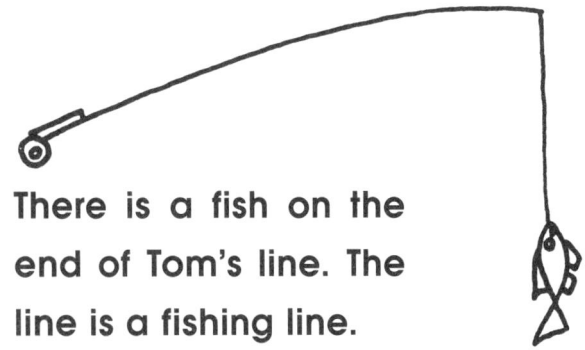

There is a fish on the end of Tom's line. The line is a fishing line.

a b c d e f g h i j k l m n o p q r s t u v w x y z

Now one of the man's feet is in the water. It is wet. His other foot is in the boat. It is not wet.

Tom is on the sand.
His legs are not wet.

Ann is in the boat. Her right shoe is off. It is in her hand. Her left shoe is on her foot.

Here are the three on the island.

There is a hole at the foot of this old tree. There are stones and bones in the hole.

There is no water on the island. Here is a bottle of water in Tom's hand.

a b c d e f g h i j k l m n o p q r s t u v w x y z

This is a glass of water.

There is water in the glass.

Now it is in Ann's hand.

There is no water in it

now. There was water in it.

There is some water in the

man's glass and in Tom's.

---

a b c d e f g h i j k l m n o p q r s t u v w x y z

Now Tom and Ann are in Tom's room.

What are those things on the shelf?

Those are shells and other things from the island.

This is a shell.

This is a sea bird's egg.

These are eggshells.

a b c d e f g h i j k l m n o p q r s t u v w x y z

Here are two animals with a stone wall between them. One is in one field and the other is in another field.

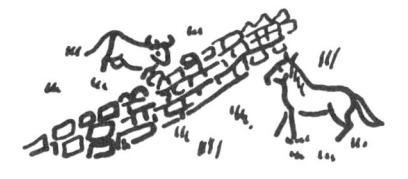

The animal on the left of the wall is a cow. The one on the right of the wall is a horse.

There are horns on the cow's head.

abcdefghijklmnopqrstuvwxyz

Now the horse and the cow are in the same field. There are some other cows in that field.

The wall between the fields is low here. Some stones are off the wall. Three of them are on the grass.

abcdefghijklmnopqrstuvwxyz

This is a flower.

There are flowers in this flower bed. A flower bed is a bed of flowers or a bed for flowers.

There is a white cat in the flower bed. There is a hole in the earth. The cat's front feet are in the hole.

Tom's hand is on his dog's collar.

a b c d e f g h i j k l m n o p q r s t u v w x y z

Where is the dog's collar? It is in Tom's hand.

Where is the dog?
It is at the foot of
a tree.

Where is the cat?
The cat is in the tree.
It is on a branch of the tree.

a b c d e f g h i j k l m n o p q r s t u v w x y z

Here is Tom in his room.

There is a comb in his hand. There are two brushes on the table. The brushes are Tom's hairbrushes. That is a glass on the wall. Is that Tom's face in the glass?

These are combs.

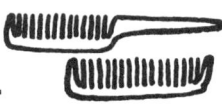

This is a brush.

abcdefghijklmnopqrstuvwxyz

Here is Tom's coat.

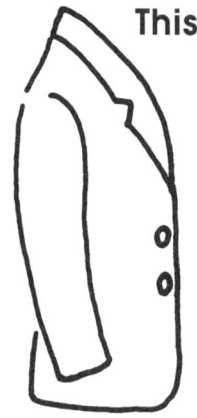

This is the collar of the coat.

These are buttons of the coat.

This is a buttonhole.

Here is a button on the floor. It is a button from Tom's coat. It is a button off the coat.

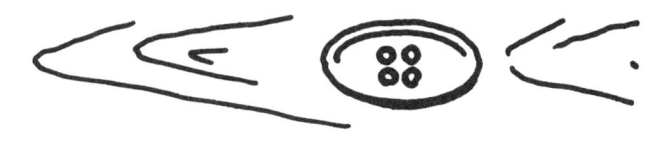

abcdefghijklmnopqrstuvwxyz

Here are the
Smiths at
the table.

There is no food on the table now. There will be food on it. The table is round.

Here is Tom's face. His mouth is under his nose. Under his mouth is his chin.

Our mouths are under our noses. Under our mouths are our chins.

abcdefghijklmnopqrstuvwxyz

This is a round table.

There are bread and butter and cake on the table. There are a bread knife and a butter knife.

This bread is white.

This bread is brown.

This is a cake.

It is a round cake.

---

a b c d e f g h i j k l m n o p q r s t u v w x y z

Here is a brown and white cow.

A man is milking the cow.

What is this?

It is milk.

It is cow's milk.

It is milk from the cow.

Those are horns on the cow's head.

abcdefghijklmnopqrstuvwxyz

Here is a glass of milk. It is in a girl's hand. The girl is the man's daughter. The man is her father. Now there is no milk in the glass.

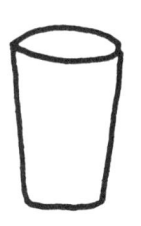

This is a bottle of milk.

Milk is good food. There is milk in this bottle. Is it black? No, it is white. This mark is black. Milk is white.

a b c d e f g h i j k l m n o p q r s t u v w x y z

There is a milk cart in the street.
Those are bottles of milk at the
door of the Smiths' house.

The milkman's horse's nose is in
a bag. There is food
for the horse in his
food bag.

abcdefghijklmnopqrstuvwxyz

It is cold in the street. There is ice on the roof of the Smiths' house. This is ice.

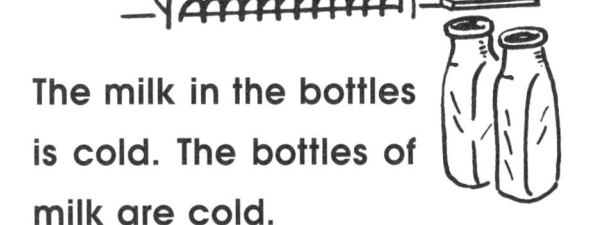

The milk in the bottles is cold. The bottles of milk are cold.

Milk is good food for us. Bread and butter and milk are good food.

abcdefghijklmnopqrstuvwxyz

Is that the sun?

Yes, it is.

Is it on the earth? No, it is not on the earth. It is in the sky.

The sun is yellow. The sky is blue. The grass is green.

The light of the sun is bright.

The clouds in the sky are white and gray.

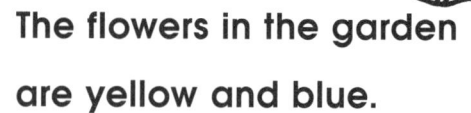

The flowers in the garden are yellow and blue.

abcdefghijklmnopqrstuvwxyz

What is this? It is a baby in its bed. Is it a boy or a girl? Yes, it is one or the other.

Is it a girl? No.

Is it a boy? Yes.

He is in his bed in the sun. His mother is in the garden with her son. She is not in the sun but he is.

abcdefghijklmnopqrstuvwxyz

Here is the sea.

There is sunlight on the sea.

There are no clouds in the sky.

Is it night or day? It is day.

Why is it day? The sun is in the sky. That is why.

Now the sun is high in the sky but it is under a cloud. There is no sunlight on the sea.

a b c d e f g h i j k l m n o p q r s t u v w x y z

Days are light.
Nights are dark.

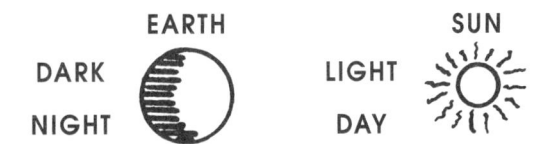

DARK NIGHT — EARTH

LIGHT DAY — SUN

When there is light on one side of the earth, the other side is dark. When the moon is in the sky, then the night is not so dark.

There is moonlight on the sea now.

a b c d e f g h i j k l m n o p q r s t u v w x y z

This is a bird.

It is a baby bird.

Its egg is broken.

The mother bird is on the other eggs. They are not broken.

There were five eggs under the mother bird. One baby is out of its egg now. Now there are four eggs under the mother bird.

---

a b c d e f g h i j k l m n o p q r s t u v w x y z

I was a baby. You were a baby.

We were babies.

He was a baby.

She was a baby.

. . . . .

All men and women and

boys and girls were babies.

They were babies.

Are you a man or a woman

or a boy or a girl?

---

abcdefghijklmnopqrstuvwxyz

This is a school. The boys and girls are at school. They are outside the school now. There is a clock over the door of the school and a bell over the clock.

Here is the bell.

abcdefghijklmnopqrstuvwxyz

Here they are in a room inside the school.

It is Monday.

There are seven days in a week: Sunday, Monday, Tuesday, Wednesday, Thursday, Friday, Saturday.

There are five school days. Saturday and Sunday are not school days.

---

a b c d e f g h i j k l m n o p q r s t u v w x y z

In Tom's face there is one (1) mouth.

On his body are two (2) arms.

On his coat are three (3) buttons.

On his cart are four (4) wheels.

On his foot are five (5) toes.

---

abcdefghijklmnopqrstuvwxyz

Here is a box.

It is a box of eggs.

There are six (6) eggs

in this box.

Now the eggs are

not in the box.

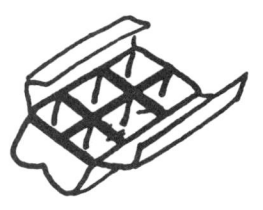

There are no eggs in it.

It is a box for eggs.

It is a box for six eggs.

There were six eggs in it.

Now the six eggs are out

of the box. $O\ O\ O\ O\ O\ O$

---

a b c d e f g h i j k l m n o p q r s t u v w x y z

Here are seven (7) stars.

Here are eight (8) fingers.

Here are nine (9) cats.

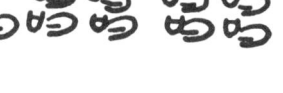

Here are ten (10) toes.

Here are eleven (11) men.

Here are twelve (12) numbers.

---

abcdefghijklmnopqrstuvwxyz

Now it is twelve.

This is the face of the clock over the school door. Those are the two hands of the clock. They are together at twelve.

The boys and girls are out of school. They were in school for three hours. They were in school from nine to twelve. Now they are all outside again.

---

a b c d e f g h i j k l m n o p q r s t u v w x y z

Here is the face of the
school clock at nine.
The short hand is at nine.

Here it is at ten.
Where is the short hand now?
Now it is eleven on the
clock. The short hand is
at eleven.
What is the time now?
It is twelve.

abcdefghijklmnopqrstuvwxyz

Now the boys and girls are in school again. What time is it?

Here is the face of the school clock. The clock is at two.

Where is the long hand and where is the short hand? What are the numbers around the face of the clock?

---

a b c d e f g h i j k l m n o p q r s t u v w x y z

Tom and Ann are at the table with their mother and their father.

There are two cups and two glasses on the table. There are five knives and spoons.

This is a knife
and this is a spoon.
This is a cup.

---

a b c d e f g h i j k l m n o p q r s t u v w x y z

Here is a plate with

a cake on it

and here

is a cake knife.

Here are three small plates.

Here is a pot.

It is a coffeepot.

Here is sugar.

And here is milk.

There is milk in the glasses.

There is coffee in the cups.

a b c d e f g h i j k l m n o p q r s t u v w x y z

This is a morning in spring.

Tom and Ann are with their grandfather. He is their mother's father.
The three are in the woods.
Tom and Ann are young.
Their grandfather is old.

---

a b c d e f g h i j k l m n o p q r s t u v w x y z

There are new young green leaves on the branches of the trees.

There are flowers under the trees. Some are blue and some are white and others are yellow.

abcdefghijklmnopqrstuvwxyz

Here is a plant.

Here is its flower.

This is a leaf.

It is one of its

leaves.

This is the stem

of the plant.

These are its

roots. Here

is one root

and here is another.

The roots are in the earth.

---

a b c d e f g h i j k l m n o p q r s t u v w x y z

This is a seed.

It is the seed of a

tree. The tree from

this seed will be an oak tree.

This is a leaf

from an oak tree.

This is a

seed of another

tree. There are

wings on this seed.

Here it is

in the air.

---

a b c d e f g h i j k l m n o p q r s t u v w x y z

There are seven days in a week.

What are their names?

They are　Sunday　　　1

　　　　　Monday　　　2

　　　　　Tuesday　　　3

　　　　　Wednesday　4

　　　　　Thursday　　5

　　　　　Friday　　　　6

　　　　　Saturday　　7

There are four weeks in a month.

There are twelve months in a year.

---

a b c d e f g h i j k l m n o p q r s t u v w x y z

In the first week of the year 2006, the first day was Sunday.

SUNDAY

MONDAY

TUESDAY

WEDNESDAY

THURSDAY

FRIDAY

SATURDAY

January 2006

Sun.	1st
Mon.	2nd
Tues.	3rd
Wed.	4th
Thur.	5th
Fri.	6th
Sat.	7th

It was the first day of the year and of the month. The first letter of 'January' is a 'j'.

---

a b c d e f g h i j k l m n o p q r s t u v w x y z

The first day of the year 2006 was a Sunday. It was the first of January. The second of January was a Monday. The third was a Tuesday and the fourth was a Wednesday.

What was the fifth?

What was the sixth?

JAN	
SUN.	1
MON.	2
TUES.	3
WED.	4

Was the seventh a Saturday?

---

a b c d e f g h i j k l m n o p q r s t u v w x y z

In 2005 the first of January was a Saturday.

In 2004 the first of January was a Thursday.

In 2003 it was a Wednesday.

In 2002 it was a Tuesday.

In 2050 it will be a Saturday.

---

a b c d e f g h i j k l m n o p q r s t u v w x y z

What day of the week is between Tuesday and Thursday? This is a question and this is a question mark.

What is the answer to this question? The answer is "Wednesday." Wednesday is the day of the week between Tuesday and Thursday. It is the day after Tuesday and before Thursday.

Question marks are the marks at the ends of questions.

---

a b c d e f g h i j k l m n o p q r s t u v w x y z

Which are the questions on this page?

There are seven days in a week.

Are there four weeks in a month?

Yes, there are.

Are there twelve months in a year?

Yes, there are twelve months in a year.

---

a b c d e f g h i j k l m n o p q r s t u v w x y z

There are twelve months in a year. Some of the months are shorter than others. Some of them are longer than others. Which is the shortest month? Which are the longest months? What are the names of the twelve months of the year?

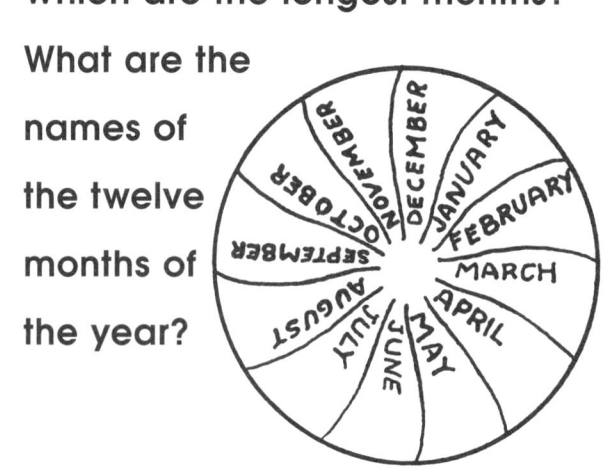

abcdefghijklmnopqrstuvwxyz

FIRST STEPS IN READING ENGLISH

	10 20 30		28 30 31
JANUARY		31	
FEBRUARY		28(9)	
MARCH		31	
APRIL		30	
MAY		31	
JUNE		30	
JULY		31	
AUGUST		31	
SEPTEMBER		30	
OCTOBER		31	
NOVEMBER		30	
DECEMBER		31	

abcdefghijklmnopqrstuvwxyz

March, April and May are the spring months. April is the month between March and May. It is the month after March and before May. March is the month before April and May is the month after. There are thirty days in April. Is it shorter than March and May? Yes. There are thirty-one days in March and May.

MARCH
APRIL
MAY

abcdefghijklmnopqrstuvwxyz

Here is a young plant in April.
Its new leaves are green. Its roots are in the wet earth. There is rain falling on it.

The plant was a seed in March.
It is small now but it will be a tall plant in May.

There will be flowers on it then.

a b c d e f g h i j k l m n o p q r s t u v w x y z

September, October and November are the autumn months.

October is the month between September and November.

There are thirty-one days in October. Is it shorter than September and November? No. There are thirty days in September and November.

```
SEPTEMBER  ———|10——|20——|30
OCTOBER    ———|10——|20——|31
NOVEMBER   ———|10——|20——|30
```

abcdefghijklmnopqrstuvwxyz

This is a morning in autumn.

There are leaves falling from the trees. There are leaves under the trees. They are yellow and red and brown. Autumn is the time of the fall of the leaves.

Tom and Ann and their grandfather are not in the woods now. There is no one in the woods.

---

a b c d e f g h i j k l m n o p q r s t u v w x y z

Autumn is the fall of the year. It is the time of the falling of leaves. In the fall every day is shorter than the day before. Every night is longer than the night before.

The sun is in the sky longer in September than in November.

abcdefghijklmnopqrstuvwxyz

In spring the year is young. It is the time of new young plants and flowers. In the spring every day is longer than the day before. Every night is shorter.

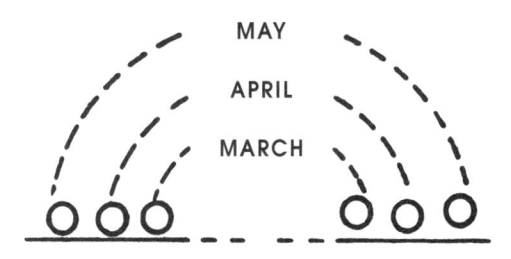

The sun is in the sky longer in May than in March.

---

a b c d e f g h i j k l m n o p q r s t u v w x y z

The summer months are June, July and August. Summer is between spring and autumn.

The winter months are December, January and February. Winter is after autumn but it is before spring.

abcdefghijklmnopqrstuvwxyz

There are three months in spring. There are three months in autumn, which is the fall of the year. Fall is after summer but before winter.

Are there four threes in twelve? Yes.

There are twelve months in every year.

---

a b c d e f g h i j k l m n o p q r s t u v w x y z

What is this?

It is a

birthday cake.

It is Tom's birthday.

"How old are you, Tom?"

That is a question.

"I am seven years old."

That is Tom's answer.

When is your birthday?

How old are you?

Those are other questions.

Tom's birthday is the fourth

day of December.

---

abcdefghijklmnopqrstuvwxyz

Tom is reading.

What is this animal?

It is a zebra, marked

ABRACADEEBRA, the Zebra

of Zee.

It is the zebra in Tom's book.

---

abcdefghijklmnopqrstuvwxyz

What is this?

It is a letter for Miss Hester Hart. Her name is on it. The letter is from Sam Sims in Zanzibar.

Here is Hester reading her letter. That is Sam's writing.

---

abcdefghijklmnopqrstuvwxyz

What is Nat Tedder reading?

He is reading the newspaper.

What is Ernest Sands reading?
He is reading a play.

*"Twelfth Night
or
What You Will"
by
William Shakespeare*

abcdefghijklmnopqrstuvwxyz

LETTER INTAKE of
FIRST STEPS IN READING ENGLISH

page

   1.......a h i m n s t
   4.......e
  12.......d
  20.......r
  40.......o
  54.......w
  70.......g
  78.......b
  82.......l
  94.......f
100.......c
104.......u
107.......k
112.......y
116.......v
121.......x
126.......p
133.......j
136.......q
149.......z

INDEX

a, A

a (an) 1
after 136
again 85
air 29
all 117
am 148
and 14
animal (-s) 90
another 48
answer 136
are 20
arm (-s) 22
around 125
ash 39
at 48
autumn 142

b, B

baby (babies) 113

bag 86
ball 88
bath 79
bathroom 78
be 85
bed (-s) 78
bedroom 78
before 136
bell 118
between 78
bird (-s, -'s) 84
birthday 148
black 109
blue 112
boat (-s) 92
body 120
bone (-s) 81
book 149
bottle (-s) 97
box 121
boy (-s) 113

branch (-es)............. 103	collar....................... 102
bread........................ 86	comb (-s)................ 104
bright...................... 112	cow (-s, -'s) 100
broken..................... 116	cup (-s).................... 126
brother 80	
brown 107	
brush (-es)............... 104	**d, D**
but............................. 75	dark 115
butter 107	daughter................. 109
button (-s)............... 105	day (-s).................... 114
buttonhole.............. 105	dog (-s, -'s)................ 70
	door (-s).................... 48
	dress (-es)................. 53
c, C	
cake 107	
cart 110	**e, E**
cat (-s,-'s) 102	ear (-s)....................... 22
chin (-s) 106	earth 57
clock 118	egg (-s) 84
cloud (-s)................. 112	eggshell..................... 99
coat 105	end 90
coffee 127	every....................... 144
coffeepot................ 127	
cold......................... 111	

f, F

face	104
fall	143
falling	141
father	109
field (-s)	100
finger (-s)	122
fish	95
fishing	95
floor	105
flower (-s)	102
food	106
foot (feet)	96
for	102
from	99
front	102

g, G

garden	72
girl (-s, 's)	88
glass (-es)	98
goat (-s, -s')	90
good	74
grandfather	128
grass	72
gray	112
green	73

h, H

hair (-s)	28
hairbrush	104
hand (-s)	12
hat (-s)	1
he	6
head (-s)	13
her	23
here	24
hers	27
high	114
his	1
hole	97
horn (-s)	91
horse (-s, -'s, -s')	46
hour (-s)	123
house	110
how	148

i, I

I	117
ice	111
in	10
inside	75
is	1
island (-s)	94
it	2
its	28

j, J

k, K

knife (knives)	107

l, L

leaf (leaves)	129
left	96
leg (-s)	83
letter (-s)	82
light	112
line	90
long	83
longer, longest	138
low	101

m, M

man (-'s)	1
men (-'s)	21
mark	109
marked	149
milk	108
milking	108
milkman (-'s)	110
month (-s)	132
moon	55
moonlight	115
morning	73
mother (-'s)	43
mouth (-s)	106

n, N

name (-s)	4
near	60
new	68

INDEX

newspaper 151
night (-s) 71
no 46
nose (-s) 45
not 42
now 54
number (-s) 122

o, O

oak 131
of 94
off 96
old 82
on 40
one 51
or 102
other (-s) 52
our 106
out 116
outside 118
over 118

p, P

page 137
plant (-s) 130
plate (-s) 127
play 151
pot 127

q, Q

question (-s) 136

r, R

rain 33
rat (-s, -s') 28
reading 149
red 80
right 79
road 61
roadside 61
roof 111
room 47
root (-s) 130
round 106

s, S

same	38
sand	77
school	118
sea	60
seat (-s)	20
seed	131
she	7
shelf	99
shell (-s)	99
shirt	49
shoe (-s)	52
short	83
shorter, shortest	138
side	49
sister (-s)	36
sky	112
small	89
smooth	74
snow	71
snowman	71
so	115
some	55
son (-'s)	42
spoon (-s)	126
spring	128
star (-s)	55
station	46
stem	130
stone (-s)	81
store	68
street (-s)	60
sugar	127
summer	146
sun	112
sunlight	114

t, T

table	104
tail (-s)	83
tall	89
than	138
that	3
the	16
their	26
them	63
then	115

Index

there	24
these	20
they	116
thing (-s)	80
this	1
those	41
time	124
to	61
toe (-s)	120
together	74
tooth (teeth)	44
town	60
train	32
tree (-s)	39

u, U
under	106
us	111

w, W
wall	88
warm	73
was	58
water	76
we	117
week (-s)	119
were	116
wet	75
what	57
wheel (-s)	120
when	115
where	58
which	137
white	70
who	59
why	114
wide	75
will	85
window (-s)	54
wing (-s)	92
winter	71
with	54
woman (women)	54
woods	128
word (-s)	69
writing	150

y, Y

year (-s)	132
yellow	112
yes	112
you	117
young	128
your	148

z, Z

zebra	149

Miss	36
Mr.	34
Mrs.	35

NUMBERS

one	51
two	54
three (-s)	31
four	116
five	116
six	121
seven	119
eight	79
nine	39
ten	51
eleven	122
twelve	122
thirty	140
thirty-one	140
first	133
second	134
third	134
fourth	134
fifth	134
sixth	134
seventh	134

MONTHS
OF THE YEAR

January	133
February	139
March	139
April	139
May	139
June	139
July	139
August	139
September	139
October	139
November	139
December	139

DAYS
OF THE WEEK

Sunday	119
Monday	119
Tuesday	119
Wednesday	119
Thursday	119
Friday	119
Saturday	119

Word List

- 本文で使われている全ての語を掲載しています（LEVEL 1、2）。ただし、LEVEL 3以上は、中学校レベルの語を含みません。
- 語形が規則変化する語の見出しは原形で示しています。不規則変化語は本文中で使われている形になっています。
- 一般的な意味を紹介していますので、一部の語で本文で実際に使われている品詞や意味と合っていないことがあります。
- 品詞は以下のように示しています。

名 名詞	代 代名詞	形 形容詞	副 副詞	動 動詞	助 助動詞
前 前置詞	接 接続詞	間 間投詞	冠 冠詞	略 略語	俗 俗語
頭 接頭語	尾 接尾語	記 記号	関 関係代名詞		

A

- **a** 冠 ①1つの, 1人の, ある ②〜につき
- **Abracadeebra** 名 アブラカデーブラ《呪文や魔除けに唱える》, 呪文
- **after** 前 〜の後に[で], の after all 結局 After you. どうぞお先に。 one after another 次々に 副 後に[で] 接 （〜した）後に[で]
- **again** 副 再び, もう一度
- **air** 名 ①《the –》空中, 空間 ②空気, 《the –》大気 ③雰囲気, 様子 in the air 空中に
- **all** 形 すべての 代 全部, すべて（のもの[人]） not ~ at all 少しも[全然]〜ない 名 全体 副 まったく, すっかり all right よろしい, 申し分ない
- **am** 動 〜である, （〜に）いる[ある]《主語がIのときのbeの現在形》
- **an** 冠 ①1つの, 1人の, ある ②〜につき
- **and** 接 ①そして, 〜と… ②《同じ語を結んで》ますます ③《結果を表して》それで, だから and so on 〜など
- **animal** 名 動物 形 動物の
- **Ann Smith** アン・スミス《人名》

- **another** 形 ①もう1つ[1人]の ②別の 代 ①もう1つ[1人] ②別のもの one another お互いに
- **answer** 動 ①答える, 応じる ②《– for》〜の責任を負う 名 答え, 応答, 返事
- **April** 名 4月
- **are** 動 〜である, （〜に）いる[ある]《主語がyou, we, theyまたは複数名詞のときのbeの現在形》 名 アール《面積単位。100平方メートル》
- **arm** 名 ①腕 ②腕状のもの, 腕木, ひじかけ ③《-s》武器, 兵器 動 武装する[させる]
- **around** 副 ①まわりに, あちこちに ②およそ, 約 前 〜のまわりに, 〜のあちこちに
- **ash** 名 ①灰, 燃えかす ②《-es》遺骨, なきがら ③トネリコ《植物》
- **at** 前 ①《場所・時》〜に[で] ②《目標・方向》〜に[を], 〜に向かって
- **August** 名 8月
- **autumn** 名 秋

B

- **baby** 名 ①赤ん坊 ②《呼びかけで》

WORD LIST

あなた 形①赤ん坊の ②小さな
- **bag** 名袋, かばん 動袋に入れる, つかまえる
- **ball** 名ボール, 球 動丸くなる, 丸める
- **bath** 名入浴, 風呂, 浴槽 動入浴する[させる]
- **bathroom** 名①浴室 ②手洗い, トイレ
- **be** 動~である, (~に)いる[ある], ~となる 助①《現在分詞とともに用いて》~している ②《過去分詞とともに用いて》~される, ~されている
- **bed** 名①ベッド, 寝所 ②花壇, 川床, 土台 go to bed 床につく, 寝る
- **bedroom** 名寝室
- **before** 前~の前に[で], ~より以前に 接~する前に 副以前に
- **bell** 名ベル, 鈴, 鐘 動①(ベル・鐘が)鳴る ②ベル[鈴]をつける
- **between** 前(2つのもの)の間に[で・の] 副間に
- **bird** 名鳥
- **birthday** 名誕生日
- **black** 形黒い, 有色の 名黒, 黒色
- **blue** 形①青い ②青ざめた ③憂うつな, 陰気な 名青(色)
- **boat** 名ボート, 小舟, 船 動ボートに乗る[乗せる], ボートで行く
- **body** 名①体, 死体, 胴体 ②団体, 組織 ③主要部, (文書の)本文
- **bone** 名①骨, 《-s》骨格 ②《-s》要点, 骨組み 動(魚・肉の)骨をとる
- **book** 名①本, 書物 ②《the B-》聖書 ③《-s》帳簿 動①記入する, 記帳する ②予約する
- **bottle** 名瓶, ボトル 動瓶に入れる[詰める]
- **box** 名①箱, 容器 ②観覧席 ③詰所 動①箱に入れる[詰める] ②ボクシングをする
- **boy** 名①少年, 男の子 ②給仕

- **branch** 名①枝 ②支流, 支部 動枝を広げる, 枝分かれする
- **bread** 名①パン ②食物, 生計
- **bright** 形①輝いている, 鮮明な ②快活な ③利口な 副輝いて, 明るく
- **broken** 動break(壊す)の過去分詞 形①破れた, 壊れた ②落胆した
- **brother** 名①兄弟 ②同僚, 同胞
- **brown** 形①茶色の ②浅黒い肌の, 日焼けした 名①茶色(のもの) ②浅黒い肌の人 動茶色にする, 日焼けする[させる]
- **brush** 名①ブラシ ②絵筆 動ブラシをかける, 払いのける
- **but** 接①でも, しかし ②~を除いて 前~を除いて, ~のほかは 副ただ, のみ, ほんの
- **butter** 名バター 動バターを塗る, バターで味をつける
- **button** 名ボタン, ボタン状の物 動ボタンをつける[かける]
- **buttonhole** 名ボタン穴

C

- **cake** 名①菓子, ケーキ ②固まり 動固まる
- **cart** 名荷馬車, 荷車 動運ぶ
- **cat** 名ネコ(猫)
- **chin** 名あご
- **clock** 名掛け[置き]時計
- **cloud** 名①雲, 雲状のもの, 煙 ②大群 動曇る, 暗くなる
- **coat** 名①コート ②(動物の)毛 動①表面を覆う ②上着を着せる
- **coffee** 名コーヒー
- **coffeepot** 名コーヒーポット
- **cold** 形①寒い, 冷たい ②冷淡な, 冷静な 名①寒さ, 冷たさ ②風邪
- **collar** 名①えり ②首輪
- **comb** 名くし 動(髪を)くしで梳く

First Steps in Reading English

- □ **content** 名①《-s》中身, 内容, 目次 ②満足 形満足して 動満足する[させる]
- □ **cow** 名雌牛, 乳牛
- □ **cup** 名①カップ, 茶わん ②賞杯, 競技大会

D

- □ **dark** 形①暗い, 闇の ②(色が)濃い ③陰うつな 名①《the-》暗がり, 闇 ②日暮れ, 夜 ③暗い色[影]
- □ **daughter** 名娘
- □ **day** 名①日中, 昼間 ②日, 期日 ③《-s》時代, 生涯
- □ **December** 名12月
- □ **diamond** 名①ダイヤモンド ②ひし形 ③《D-》ダイヤモンド《名前》
- □ **dog** 名犬
- □ **door** 名①ドア, 戸 ②一軒, 一戸
- □ **dress** 名ドレス, 衣服, 正装 動①服を着る[着せる] ②飾る

E

- □ **ear** 名耳, 聴覚 **be all ears** 熱心に聞く
- □ **earth** 名①《the-》地球 ②大地, 陸地, 土 ③この世 **on earth** 世界中で, 地上で,《疑問・否定文で》いったい全体, およそ
- □ **egg** 名卵
- □ **eggshell** 名①卵の殻 ②砕けやすいもの
- □ **eight** 名8(の数字), 8人[個] 形8の, 8人[個]の
- □ **eleven** 名①11(の数字), 11人[個] ②11人のチーム, イレブン 形11の, 11人[個]の
- □ **end** 名①終わり, 終末, 死 ②果て, 末, 端 ③目的 **in the end** とうとう, 最後には 動終わる, 終える
- □ **English** 名①英語 ②《the-》英国人 形①英語の ②英国(人)の
- □ **Enid Hart** エニド・ハート《人名》
- □ **Ernest Sands** アーネスト・サンズ《人名》
- □ **Esther Hart** エスター・ハート《人名》
- □ **every** 形①どの~も, すべての, あらゆる ②毎~, ~ごとの

F

- □ **face** 名①顔, 顔つき ②外観, 外見 ③(時計の)文字盤, (建物の)正面 **face to face** 面と向かって, 差し向かいで **in (the) face of ~** ~の面前で, ~に直面して 動直面する, 立ち向かう
- □ **fall** 動①落ちる, 倒れる ②(値段・温度が)下がる 名①落下, 転落 ②滝 ③崩壊 ④秋
- □ **falling** 名落下, 崩落
- □ **father** 名①父親 ②先祖, 創始者 ③《F-》神 ④神父, 司祭
- □ **February** 名2月
- □ **feet** 名①foot(足)の複数 ②フィート《長さの単位。約30cm》
- □ **field** 名①野原, 田畑, 広がり ②(研究)分野 ③競技場
- □ **fifth** 名第5番目(の人[物]), 5日 形第5番目の
- □ **finger** 名(手の)指 動指でさわる
- □ **first** 名最初, 第1(の人[物]) **at first** 最初は, 初めのうちは 形①第1の, 最初の ②最も重要な 副第一に, 最初に **first of all** 何よりもまず
- □ **fish** 名魚 動釣りをする
- □ **fishing** 名魚釣り, 漁業
- □ **five** 名5(の数字), 5人[個] 形5の, 5人[個]の
- □ **floor** 名床, 階

166

WORD LIST

- **flower** 名①花, 草花 ②満開 **flower bed** 花壇 動花が咲く

- **food** 名食物, えさ, 肥料

- **foot** 名①足, 足取り ②(山などの)ふもと ③フィート《長さの単位。約30cm》

- **for** 前①《目的・原因・対象》～にとって, ～のために[の], ～に対して ②《期間》～間 ③《代理》～の代わりに ④《方向》～へ(向かって)

- **four** 名4(の数字), 4人[個] **on all fours** 四つんばいになって 形4の, 4人[個]の

- **fourth** 名第4番目(の人・物), 4日 形第4番目の

- **Friday** 名金曜日

- **from** 前①《出身・出発点・時間・順序・原料》～から ②《原因・理由》～がもとで

- **front** 名正面, 前 形正面の, 前面の

G

- **garden** 名庭, 庭園 動園芸をする, 庭いじりをする

- **girl** 名女の子, 少女

- **glass** 名①ガラス(状のもの), コップ, グラス ②鏡, 望遠鏡 ③《-es》めがね

- **goat** 名ヤギ(山羊)

- **good** 形よい, 上手な, 優れた **as good as ～** ～も同然で, ほとんど～ **be good at ～** ～が得意である 間よかった, わかった, よろしい 名善, 徳, 益, 幸福

- **grandfather** 名祖父

- **grass** 名草, 牧草(地), 芝生 動草[芝生]で覆う[覆われる]

- **gray** 形①灰色の ②どんよりした, 憂うつな 名灰色 動灰色になる[する]

- **green** 形①緑色の, 青々とした ②未熟な, 若い ③生き生きした ④生の, 未加工の 名①緑色 ②草地, 芝生, 野菜

H

- **hair** 名髪, 毛

- **hairbrush** 名ヘアブラシ

- **hand** 名①手 ②(時計の)針 ③援助の手, 助け **at hand** 近くに, 近づいて **hand in hand** 手をつないで **on hand** 手元に **on the other hand** 他方では 動手渡す **hand in** 差し出す, 提出する **hand out** 配る **hand over** 引き渡す, 譲渡する

- **hat** 名(縁のある)帽子

- **he** 代彼は[が]

- **head** 名①頭 ②先頭 ③長, 指導者 動向かう, 向ける

- **her** 代①彼女を[に] ②彼女の

- **here** 副①ここに[で] ②《Here is [are] ～》ここに～がある ③さあ, そら **Here it is.** はい, どうぞ。 **Here we are.** さあ着きました。 **Here you are.** はい, どうぞ。 **Look here.** ほら。ねえ。 名ここ

- **hers** 代彼女のもの

- **Hester Hart** ヘスター・ハート《人名》

- **high** 形①高い ②気高い, 高価な 副①高く ②ぜいたくに 名高い所

- **his** 代①彼の ②彼のもの

- **hole** 名①穴, すき間 ②苦境, 困難 動穴をあける, 穴に入る[入れる]

- **horn** 名①(牛・羊などの)角, 角材, (楽器の)ホルン

- **horse** 名馬

- **hour** 名①1時間, 時間

- **house** 名①家, 家庭 ②(特定の目的のための)建物, 小屋

- **how** 副①どうやって, どれくらい, どんなふうに ②なんて(～だろう)

③《関係副詞》～する方法 **How do you like ～?** ～はどう思いますか。～はいかがですか。

I

- [ ] **I** 代 私は[が]
- [ ] **ice** 名 ①氷 ②氷菓子 動 凍る，凍らす，氷で冷やす
- [ ] **Ida Reed** アイダ・リード《人名》
- [ ] **in** 前 ①《場所・位置・所属》～(の中) に[で・の] ②《時》～(の時) に[の・で]，～後(に)，～の間(に) ③《方法・手段》～で ④～を身につけて，～を着て 副 中へ[に]，内へ[に]
- [ ] **index** 名 ①索引 ②しるし，現れ ③指数
- [ ] **inside** 名 内部，内側 **inside out** 裏返しに，ひっくり返して 形 内部[内側]にある 副 内部[内側]に 前 ～の内部[内側]に
- [ ] **intake** 名 取り入れ(口)，吸い込み
- [ ] **is** 動 be (～である)の3人称単数現在
- [ ] **island** 名 島
- [ ] **it** 代 ①それは[が]，それを[に] ②《天候・日時・距離・寒暖などを示す》
- [ ] **its** 代 それの，あれの

J

- [ ] **January** 名 1月
- [ ] **July** 名 7月
- [ ] **June** 名 6月

K

- [ ] **knife** 名 ナイフ，小刀，包丁，短剣
- [ ] **knives** 名 knife (ナイフ)の複数

L

- [ ] **leaf** 名 葉
- [ ] **leaves** 名 leaf (葉)の複数 動 leave (出発する)の3人称単数現在
- [ ] **left** 名 《the -》左，左側 形 左の，左側の 副 左に，左側に 動 leave (出発する)の過去，過去分詞
- [ ] **leg** 名 ①脚，すね ②支柱
- [ ] **letter** 名 ①手紙 ②文字 ③文学，文筆業
- [ ] **light** 名 光，明かり **come to light** 明るみに出る 動 火をつける，照らす，明るくする 形 ①明るい ②(色が)薄い，淡い ③軽い，容易な **make light of ～** ～を軽んじる 副 軽く，容易に
- [ ] **line** 名 ①線，糸，電話線 ②(字の)行 ③列，(電車の)～線 動 ①線を引く ②整列する
- [ ] **list** 名 一覧表，目録 動 ～を(表・名簿などに)記載する
- [ ] **long** 形 長い，長期の 副 長い間，ずっと **no longer ～** もはや～でない[～しない] **not ～ any longer** もはや～でない[～しない] **so [as] long as ～** ～する限りは 名 長い期間 **before long** 間もなく，やがて 動 切望する，思い焦がれる
- [ ] **low** 形 ①低い，弱い ②低級の，劣等な 副 低く 名 ①低い水準[点] ②低速ギア

M

- [ ] **man** 名 男性，人，人類
- [ ] **march** 名 ①行進 ②《M-》3月 動 行進する[させる]，進展する
- [ ] **mark** 名 ①印，記号，跡 ②点数 ③特色 動 ①印[記号]をつける ②採点する ③目立たせる
- [ ] **may** 助 ①～かもしれない ②～してもよい，～できる **May I ～?** ～してもよいですか? 名 《M-》5月
- [ ] **men** 名 man (男性)の複数

Word List

- **milk** 名牛乳, ミルク 動乳をしぼる
- **milkman** 名牛乳配達人
- **miss** 動①失敗する, 免れる ②(~が)ないのに気づく, (人が)いなくてさびしく思う 名①はずれ, 失敗 ②《M-》~さん, ~嬢《未婚の女性に対して用いる》
- **Monday** 名月曜日
- **month** 名月, 1か月
- **moon** 名月, 月光 new moon 新月 old moon 欠けていく月, 下弦の月
- **moonlight** 名月明かり, 月光
- **morning** 名朝, 午前
- **mother** 名母, 母親
- **mouth** 名①口 ②言葉, 発言
- **Mr.** 名《男性に対して。Mrとも》~さん, ~氏
- **Mrs.** 名《結婚している女性に対して。Mrsとも》~さん, ~夫人

N

- **name** 名①名前 ②名声 ③《-s》悪口 by name 名前で, 名前だけは call ~ names ~の悪口を言う 動①名前をつける ②名指する name after [for] ~ ~の名をとって命名する
- **Nat Tedder** ナット・テッダー《人名》
- **near** 前~の近くに, ~のそばに 形近い, 親しい 副近くに, 親密で near at hand 手近に near by 近くに[の]
- **Ned Reed** ネッド・リード《人名》
- **new** 形①新しい, 新規の ②新鮮で, できたての What's new? お変わりありませんか。
- **newspaper** 名新聞(紙)
- **night** 名夜, 晩
- **nine** 名9(の数字), 9人[個] 形9の, 9人[個]の
- **no** 副①いいえ, いや ②少しも~ない 形~がない, 少しも~ない, ~どころでない, ~禁止 名否定, 拒否
- **nose** 名鼻, 嗅覚, におい
- **not** 副~でない, ~しない not (~) at all まったく(~で)ない not ~ but… ~ではなくて… not yet まだ~してない
- **November** 名11月
- **now** 副①今(では), 現在 ②今すぐに ③では, さて right now 今すぐに, たった今 just now 今, 現在 by now 今のところ for now 当分の間, 当面は from now on 今後 形今の, 現在の
- **number** 名①数, 数字, 番号 ②~号, ~番 ③《-s》多数 a number of ~ いくつかの~, 多くの~ 動番号をつける, 数える

O

- **oak** 名オーク《ブナ科の樹木の総称》 形オーク(材)の
- **October** 名10月
- **of** 前①《所有・所属・部分》~の, ~に属する ②《性質・特徴・材料》~の, ~製の ③《部分》~のうち ④《分離・除去》~から
- **off** 副①離れて ②はずれて ③止まって ④休んで 形①離れて ②季節はずれの ③休みの 前~を離れて, ~をはずれて, (値段が)~引きの
- **old** 形①年取った, 老いた ②~歳の ③古い, 昔の 名昔, 老人
- **on** 前①《場所・接触》~(の上)に ②《日・時》~に, ~と同時に, ~のすぐ後で ③《関係・従事》~に関して, ~について, ~して ④~を支点として, ~に支えられて 副①身につけて, 上に ②前へ, 続けて
- **one** 名1(の数字), 1人[個] one by one 1つずつ, ひとりずつ 形①

169

FIRST STEPS IN READING ENGLISH

1の, 1人[個]の ②ある～ ③《the -》唯一の 代①(一般の)人, ある物 ②一方, 片方 ③～なもの

- **or** 接①～か…, または ②さもないと ③すなわち, 言い換えると

- **other** 形①ほかの, 異なった ②(2つのうち)もう一方の, (3つ以上のうち)残りの **every other ～** 1つおきの～ **the other day** 先日 代①ほかの人[物] ②《the -》残りのひとつ **one or the other** どちらか一方 副そうでなく, 別に

- **Otto** オットー《名前》

- **our** 代私たちの

- **out** 副①外へ[に], 不在で, 離れて ②世に出て ③消えて ④すっかり 形①外の, 遠く離れた, ②公表された 前～から外へ[に] 動①追い出す ②露出する ③(スポーツで)アウトにする

- **outside** 名外部, 外側 形外部の, 外側の 副外へ, 外側に 前～の外に[で・の・へ], ～の範囲を越えて

- **over** 前①～の上の[に], ～を一面に覆って ②～を越えて, ～以上に, ～よりまさって ③～の向こう側の[に] ④～の間 副①上に, 一面に, ずっと ②終わって, すんで **over and over (again)** 何度も繰り返して

P

- **page** 名①ページ ②(ホテルなどの)ボーイ 動(ボーイや放送で)呼び出す

- **Peacock Pie** 名『孔雀のパイ』《ウォルター・デ・ラ・メアの詩集》

- **plant** 名①植物, 草木 ②設備, プラント, 工場 動植えつける, すえつける

- **plate** 名①(浅い)皿, 1皿の料理 ②金属板, 標札, プレート 動めっきする, 板金をする

- **play** 動①遊ぶ, 競技する ②(楽器を)演奏する, (役を)演じる 名遊び, 競技, 劇

- **pot** 名壺, (深い)なべ 動壺に入れる, 鉢植えにする

Q

- **question** 名質問, 疑問, 問題 **come into question** 問題になる, 議論される **in question** 問題の, 論争中の 動①質問する ②調査する ③疑う

R

- **rain** 名雨, 降雨 **rain or shine** 雨でも晴れでも, どんなことがあっても 動①雨が降る ②雨のように降る[降らせる] **be rained out** (試合などが)雨で流れる

- **rat** 名①ネズミ(鼠) ②裏切り者

- **read** 動読む, 読書する **read out** 読み上げる, 声に出して読む **read over ～** ～に目を通す **read through ～** ～を読み通す

- **reading** 名①読むこと, 読書(力) ②読本

- **red** 形赤い 名赤, 赤色 **get into red** 赤字になる, 赤字を出す **in the red** 赤字で

- **right** 形①正しい ②適切な ③健全な ④右(側)の 副①まっすぐに, すぐに ②右(側)に ③ちょうど, 正確に **right away** すぐに **right now** ちょうど今 名①正しいこと ②権利 ③《the -》右, ライト ④《the R-》右翼

- **road** 名①道路, 道, 通り ②手段, 方法

- **roadside** 名道端, 路傍 形道端の

- **roof** 名屋根(のようなもの), 住居 動屋根をつける

- **room** 名①部屋 ②空間, 余地

170

WORD LIST

- **root** 名①根, 根元 ②根源, 原因 ③《-s》先祖, ルーツ **by the root(s)** 根こそぎ **take [strike] root** 根づく, 定着する 動根づかせる, 根づく

- **round** 形①丸い, 円形の ②ちょうど 副①回って ②周りに **go round** 回って行く, 行き渡る **round and round** ぐるぐると 名①円, 球, 輪 ②回転 前①~を回って ②~の周囲に 動①丸くなる[する] ②回る

S

- **Sam Sims** サム・シムズ《人名》

- **same** 形①同じ, 同様の ②前述の **the same ~ as [that]** … …と同じ(ような)~ 代《the-》同一の人[物] 副《the-》同様に

- **sand** 名①砂 ②《-s》砂漠, 砂浜

- **Saturday** 名土曜日

- **school** 名①学校, 校舎, 授業(時間) ②教習所, 学部 ③流派 ④群れ

- **sea** 名海, 《S-~》~海 **sea bird** 海鳥 **sea water** 海水

- **seat** 名いす, 席, 座席, 位置 動着席させる, すえつける

- **second** 名①第2(の人[物]) ②(時間の)秒, 瞬時 **second to none** 誰[何]にも劣らない 形第2の, 2番の 副第2に 動後援する, 支持する

- **seed** 名種 動種をまく

- **September** 名9月

- **seven** 名7(の数字), 7人[個] 形7の, 7人[個]の

- **seventh** 名第7番目(の人・物), 7日 形第7番目の

- **she** 代彼女は[が]

- **shelf** 名棚

- **shell** 名①貝がら, (木の実・卵などの)から ②(建物の)骨組み

- **shirt** 名ワイシャツ, ブラウス

- **shoe** 名《-s》靴 動(馬に)てい鉄をうつ

- **short** 形①短い ②背の低い ③不足している **be short of ~** ~が足りない 副①手短に, 簡単に ②不足して **come short of ~** ~に及ばない **cut short ~** ~を切って短くする, ~を途中でさえぎる **run short** 不足する, 切らす 名①《the-》要点 ②短編映画 ③(野球で)ショート **for short** 略して **in short** 要約すると

- **side** 名側, 横, そば, 斜面 **on the side** 副業で, 片手間に **side by side** 並んで 形①側面の, 横の ②副次的な 動(~の)側につく, 賛成する

- **sister** 名①姉妹, 姉, 妹 ②修道女

- **six** 名6(の数字), 6人[個] 形6の, 6人[個]の

- **sixth** 名第6番目(の人・物), 6日 形第6番目の

- **sky** 名①空, 天空, 大空 ②天気, 空模様, 気候

- **small** 形①小さい, 少ない ②取るに足りない 副小さく, 細かく

- **smooth** 形滑らかな, すべすべした, (水面・海が)静かな 動滑らかにする, 平らにする

- **snow** 名雪 動雪が降る

- **snowman** 名雪だるま, 雪男

- **so** 副①とても ②同様に, ~もまた ③《先行する句・節の代用》そのように, そう **not so ~ as** … …ほど~でない **~ or so** ~かそこら, ~くらい **so as to do** ~するように, ~するために **so ~ as to do** …するほど~で **so that** それゆえに **so ~ that** … あまり~なので…だ **so that ~ may [can]** … ~が…するために 接①だから, それで ②では, さて **So what?** それがどうした。どうでもいいではないか。

- **some** 形①いくつかの, 多少の ②ある, 誰か, 何か **some time** いつか, そのうち 副約, およそ 代①いくつか ②ある人[物]たち

First Steps in Reading English

- **son** 名息子, 子弟, ～の子
- **spoon** 名スプーン 動スプーンですくう
- **spring** 名①春 ②泉, 源 ③ばね, ぜんまい 動跳ねる, 跳ぶ
- **star** 名①星, 星形の物 ②人気者 形星形の
- **station** 名①駅 ②署, 局, 本部, 部署 動部署につかせる, 配置する
- **stem** 名①茎, (木の)幹 ②(ワイングラスの)柄
- **step** 名①歩み, 1歩(の距離) ②段階 ③踏み段, 階段 **step by step** 一歩一歩, 着実に 動歩む, 踏む
- **stone** 名①石, 小石 ②宝石 形石造りの
- **store** 名①店 ②蓄え **in store** 蓄えて, 用意されて **in store for ~** ～を待ち構えて 動蓄える, 貯蔵する
- **street** 名①街路 ②«S-»～通り
- **sugar** 名①砂糖 ②甘言, お世辞 動砂糖を入れる, 甘くする
- **summer** 名夏
- **sun** 名《the -》太陽, 日, 日光
- **Sunday** 名日曜日
- **sunlight** 名日光

T

- **table** 名①テーブル, 食卓, 台 ②一覧表 **on the table** 棚上げされて **set the table** 食卓の用意をする 動卓上に置く, 棚上げにする
- **tail** 名①尾, しっぽ ②後部, 末尾 動尾行する 形後ろからくる, 後部にある **tail end** 《the -》末端, 末尾
- **tall** 形高い, 背の高い
- **teeth** 名 tooth (歯) の複数
- **ten** 名10(の数字), 10人[個] **ten to one** 十中八九, 九分九厘 形10の, 10人[個]の
- **than** 接～よりも, ～以上に
- **that** 形その, あの 代①それ, あれ, その[あの]人[物] ②«関係代名詞»～である… **and that** しかも **that is (to say)** すなわち **That's it.** それだけのことだ。 **that's that** それで終わりだ 接～ということ, ～なので, ～だから 副そんなに, それほど
- **the** 冠①その, あの ②«形容詞の前で»～な人々 副«- + 比較級, - + 比較級»～すればするほど…
- **their** 代彼(女)らの, それらの
- **them** 代彼(女)らを[に], それらを[に]
- **then** 副①その時(に・は), それから, 次に (every) **now and then** 時折, 時々 名その時 形その当時の
- **there** 副①そこに[で・の], そこへ, あそこへ ②«- is[are]»～がある[いる] 名そこ
- **these** 代これら, これ 形これらの, この
- **they** 代①彼(女)らは[が], それらは[が] ②(一般の)人々は[が]
- **thing** 名①物, 事 ②«-s»事情, 事柄 ③«one's -s»持ち物, 身の回り品 ④人, やつ **for one thing** 1つには
- **third** 名第3(の人[物]) 形第3の, 3番の
- **thirty** 名30(の数字), 30人[個] 形30の, 30人[個]の
- **thirty-one** 名31(の数字), 31人[個] 形31の, 31人[個]の
- **this** 形①この, こちらの, これを ②今の, 現在の 代①これ, この人[物] ②今, ここ
- **those** 代それらの, あれらの **in those days** その当時 代それら[あれら]の人[物]
- **three** 名3(の数字), 3人[個] 形3の, 3人[個]の
- **Thursday** 名木曜日
- **Tim Smith** ティム・スミス《人名》

172

WORD LIST

- **time** 名①時, 時間, 歳月 ②時期 ③期間 ④時代 ⑤回, 倍 **all the time** ずっと, いつも **at a time** 一度に, 続けざまに **(at) any time** いつでも **at one time** かつては **at times** 時折 **behind time** 遅刻して **for a time** しばらく **for the time being** 今のところは **from time to time** 時々 **have a good time** 楽しい時を過ごす **in time** 間に合って, やがて **on time** 時間どおりに **Time is up.** もう時間だ。 動時刻を決める, 時間を計る

- **to** 前①《方向・変化》~へ, ~に, ~の方へ ②《程度・時間》~まで ③《適合・付加・所属》~に ④《 − ＋動詞の原形》~するために[の], ~する, ~すること

- **toe** 名足指, つま先

- **together** 副①一緒に, ともに ②同時に

- **Tom Smith** トム・スミス《人名》

- **tooth** 名歯, 歯状のもの

- **town** 名町, 都会, 都市

- **train** 名①列車, 電車 ②(~の)列, 連続 動訓練する, 仕立てる

- **tree** 名①木, 樹木, 木製のもの ②系図

- **Tuesday** 名火曜日

- **Twelfth Night, or What You Will** 名『十二夜』《シェイクスピアの戯曲》

- **twelve** 名12(の数字), 12人[個] 形12の, 12人[個]の

- **two** 名2(の数字), 2人[個] 形2の, 2人[個]の

U

- **under** 前①《位置》~の下[に] ②《状態》~で, ~を受けて, ~のもと ③《数量》~以下[未満]の, ~より下の 形下の, 下部の 副下に[で], 従属[服従]して

- **us** 代私たちを[に]

W

- **wall** 名①壁, 塀 ②障壁 動壁[塀]で囲む, ふさぐ

- **Walter de la Mare** ウォルター・デ・ラ・メア(1873-1956)《イギリスの詩人・小説家》

- **warm** 形①暖かい, 温暖な ②思いやりのある, 愛情のある 動暖まる, 暖める **warm up** 暖まる, ウォーミングアップする, 盛り上がる

- **was** 動《beの第1・第3人称単数現在am, isの過去》~であった, (~に)いた[あった]

- **water** 名①水 ②(川・湖・海などの)多量の水 動水を飲ませる, (植物に)水をやる **water down** 水で薄める

- **we** 代私たちは[が]

- **Wednesday** 名水曜日

- **week** 名週, 1週間

- **were** 動《beの2人称単数・複数の過去》~であった, (~に)いた[あった]

- **wet** 形ぬれた, 湿った, 雨の 動ぬらす, ぬれる

- **what** 代①何が[を・に] ②《関係代名詞》~するところのもの[こと] **What (~) for?** 何のために, なぜ **What's up?** 何があったのですか。 形①何の, どんな ②なんと ③~するだけの 副いかに, どれほど

- **wheel** 名①輪, 車輪, 《the−》ハンドル ②旋回 動①回転する[させる] ②~を押す

- **when** 副①いつ ②《関係副詞》~するところの, ~するとその時, ~する時 接~の時, ~する時 代いつ

- **where** 副①どこに[で] ②《関係副詞》~するところの, そしてそこで, ~するところ 接~なところに[へ],

173

~するところに[へ] 代①どこ, どの点 ②~するところの

- **which** 形①どちらの, どの, どれでも ②どんな~でも, そしてこの 代①どちら, どれ, どの人[物] ②《関係代名詞》~するところの
- **white** 形①白い, (顔色などが)青ざめた ②白人の 名①白, 白色
- **who** 代①誰が[は], どの人 ②《関係代名詞》~するところの(人)
- **why** 副①なぜ, どうして ②《関係副詞》~するところの(理由) **Why don't you ~?** ~しませんか。**Why not?** どうしてだめなのですか。いいですか。間①おや, まあ ②もちろん, なんだって ③ええと
- **wide** 形幅の広い, 広範囲の 副広く, 大きく開いて
- **will** 助~だろう, ~しよう, する(つもりだ) **Will you ~?** ~してくれませんか。名決意, 意図
- **William Shakespeare** ウィリアム・シェイクスピア(1564-1616)《イギリスの劇作家》
- **window** 名窓, 窓ガラス
- **wing** 名①翼, 羽 ②(花の)翼弁, (果実の)翼
- **winter** 名冬 動冬を過ごす
- **with** 前①《同伴・付随・所属》~と一緒に, ~を身につけて, ~とともに ②《様態》~(の状態)で, ~して ③《手段・道具》~で, ~を使って **with all ~** ~にもかかわらず, あれほど~があるのに
- **woman** 名(成人した)女性, 婦人
- **women** 名 woman(女性)の複数
- **wood** 名①〈-s〉森, 林 ②木材, まき
- **word** 名①語, 単語 ②ひと言 ③《one's -》約束 **in other words** 言い換えれば
- **write** 動書く, 手紙を書く **write down** 書き留める **write out** 詳しく書く, 清書する
- **writing** 名①書くこと, 執筆 ②筆跡 ③手紙, 文書

Y

- **year** 名①年, 1年 ②学年, 年度 ③~歳 **all (the) year round [around]** 一年中 **for years** 何年も
- **yellow** 形黄色の 名黄色
- **yes** 副はい, そうです 名肯定の言葉[返事]
- **you** 代①あなた(方)は[が], あなた(方)を[に] ②(一般に)人は
- **young** 形若い, 幼い, 青年の
- **your** 代あなた(方)の

Z

- **Zanzibar** 名ザンジバル《地名》
- **zebra** 名シマウマ(縞馬), ゼブラ
- **Zebra of Zee** 《the-》ジーのシマウマ《『孔雀のパイ』の中の詩に登場するシマウマ》
- **Zee** 名ジー《人名》

174

E-CAT

English **C**onversational **A**bility **T**est
国際英語会話能力検定

● E-CATとは…
英語が話せるようになるための
テストです。インターネット
ベースで、30分であなたの発
話力をチェックします。

www.ecatexam.com

iTEP

International Test of English Proficiency

● iTEP®とは…
世界各国の企業、政府機関、アメリカの大学
300校以上が、英語能力判定テストとして採用。
オンラインによる90分のテストで文法、リー
ディング、リスニング、ライティング、スピー
キングの5技能をスコア化。iTEP®は、留学、就
職、海外赴任などに必要な、世界に通用する英
語力を総合的に評価する画期的なテストです。

www.itepexamjapan.com

ラダーシリーズ
First Steps in Reading English 絵で読む英語

2006年9月1日　第1刷発行
2024年12月7日　第16刷発行

著　者　Ｉ・Ａ・リチャーズ
　　　　クリスティン・ギブソン

発行者　賀川　洋

発行所　IBCパブリッシング株式会社
　　　　〒162-0804 東京都新宿区中里町29番3号
　　　　菱秀神楽坂ビル
　　　　Tel. 03-3513-4511　Fax. 03-3513-4512
　　　　www.ibcpub.co.jp

© Language Research, Inc. 1957
© IBC Publishing, Inc. 2006

印刷　株式会社シナノパブリッシングプレス
装丁　伊藤 理恵
組版データ　ITC Avant Garde Gothic Demi + Avenir 65 Medium

落丁本・乱丁本は、小社宛にお送りください。送料小社負担にてお取り替えいたし
ます。本書の無断複写（コピー）は著作権法上での例外を除き禁じられています。

Printed in Japan
ISBN978-4-89684-298-2